OGUN

SANTERIA AND THE MASTER OF IRON

By Baba Raul Canizares

ORIGINAL PUBLICATIONS
Visit us on the WEB:
www.OCCULT1.com
Telephone: 1 (888) OCCULT-1

Ogun

SANTERIA AND THE MASTER OF IRON

ISBN: 0-942272-82-X

The author and publisher offer this book for interest, folkloric value, experimentation and whatever value it may have to the reader. Please be advised that we cannot make any claim of supernatural effects or powers for any of the methods or interpretations made herein. The book is offered as literary curio only. No responsibility whatsoever for the contents or veracity of the statements herein is assumed by the author or publisher or seller of this book.

FIRST EDITION

First Printing 2006

Cover Art and Illustrations
by Baba Raul Canizares
Frontispiece and Back Cover Art
by Eric K. Lerner

INTRODUCTION

Ogun's laughter is no joke.

His enemies scatter in all directions.

The butterflies do not have to see the leopard—

As soon as they smell his shit,

They scatter in all directions![1]

A new military governor of Ogun state, Nigeria, insisted on taking his oath of office not on the Bible or the Qur'an as was the custom in colonially introduced institutions, but on a steel cutlass, the traditional Yoruba implement for taking oaths, symbolizing Ogun as god of iron, warfare, and justice.[2] In most courtrooms in Yorubaland, people nowadays have a choice to be sworn in on a Bible, a Qur'an, or a piece of iron representing Ogun. In this manner, and in this instance, the indigenous religion is being accorded the same treatment and respect as that given to the two great imported faiths, Christianity and Islam. Ogun's status in Yorubaland (Southwestern Nigeria) has been steadily increasing over the last two centuries. In fact, modern African theologians name Ogun as one of the deities that created humankind. As Professor Abimbola states:

> [The] creation of human beings was a joint effort between Ògún who molded the skeleton, Obatàtálá (Òòsànlá) who molded clay on the skeleton, Olodùmarè who supplied the vital breath force known as Èmí, and Àjàlá who supplied Ori-inú (the inner head).[3]

Although in Cuban Santeria Ogun is not generally thought of as a creator deity, his role as the head warrior of the religion is extremely important (more on "The Warriors later"); as world-famous akpwon (praise singer) and priest of Ogun Lazaro Ros says in the Cuban-made documentary Ogun, " . . . The Warriors are the foundation stones where all other initiations in the Religion rest." One of the first so-called "secrets" I learned after my own initiation as a priest of Obatala was that, contrary to what is exoterically taught, Eleggua is not the first Orisha to partake of blood sacrifices; Ogun is. This is symbolized by the metal knife that cuts the throat of the sacrificial victim, thus "tasting" its blood first, the knife being a symbol of Ogun himself. But what of animals that are sacrificed without using a metal instrument? Since Ogun represents the life-force, any time that life-force is released in a ritualistic fashion, Ogun is said to be present.

I'll always remember my first encounter with that energy we call Ogun. A scar that covers most of my left ankle will not let me forget it! It all happened many years ago, when I was seven years old and still an iyawo (apprentice priest). During a routine reading, my Padrino, Juan Garcia, revealed that Ogun was to take my life on that day. His normally dark-ebony complexion became ashen and his calm, thoughtful manner became agitated and jittery as he seemed to be frantically trying to find a solution by throwing the okpele (divining chain) over and over. Finally, a look of relief covered his face as he communicated to my mother and me that Obatala had interceded for my life and Ogun would accept a substitute sacrifice of a black rooster instead. Soon one of Padrino's assistants showed up with the unfortunate bird that would lose its life for me. Padrino warned that although my life had been spared, I shouldn't be allowed out of the house that day, that I should stay inside and let the danger pass by.

On the way back home, Mother held on tight to me as we rode the bus back to Havana (Padrino lived in the little working-class, industrial town of Luyanó). Before the bus made a complete stop, the driver opened its front door. It was a stupid thing to do, but commonly done for reasons I do not know. Perhaps the drivers did it intentionally so that young men could show how "macho" they were by getting off the bus while the bus was still moving. It was a "fad" back in the late 50s and early 60s. I had seen my teenaged cousin do this many times, so that day I decided to do like the big boys and get off the bus while it was still moving. The motion of the bus created a vacuum that sucked me in under the bus. I ended up with my foot entirely under the old British-made Leland bus's huge front tire. The driver stepped on the brakes and didn't dare take his foot off thinking if the bus moved forward, the back tires might run me over. The bus had no reverse; as everything else from capitalist states, the British bus was falling apart, another victim of the U.S. embargo.

Finally, a group of men lifted the bus and I was pulled away by ambulance workers that had arrived on the scene. Amazingly, my foot suffered no major damage, my bones were intact (remember Ogun is said to be the creator of the skeleton), though the skin around my ankle was so badly mangled that the resulting scar has withstood the test of time, still there after nearly forty years. I was released from the hospital in about a week. Skeptics tried to say that my foot hadn't suffered more because a brand new coating of tar had been sprayed on the street, and under the hot sun it had yielded enough under the weight of the bus to save my foot. Whatever the means Ogun used to save me, I am thankful that he did.

MAFEREFUN OGUN!

1

Sacred Stories About Ogun

In Cuban Santeria, one of the most often-told, yet controversial pataki (sacred stories) involving Ogun talks about his incest with his own mother, Yemmu.

Recited in Cuba for hundreds of years, but apparently no longer told in Yorubaland, the story relates how Yemmu and her husband, Obatala, the original pair, lived in harmony with their children the Orisha and the humans who were loved by Obatala as much as if they were his children also.

Ogun was the firstborn of Yemmu and Obatala. Ogun had received from Olodumare, God Almighty, the knowledge of how to work iron; he had dominion over the forge. The eternal child, Eleggua, was not of Yemmu born, but lived with the primordial couple as if he were their youngest son. Eleggua was as old as time, but enjoyed being treated as Obatala's little boy. As Ogun grew into a strapping youth, it fell on him to care for his mother and the eternally little Eleggua whenever Obatala was gone. Obatala's guard, the one that told him all that transpired at home while he was away, was the enchanted rooster Osun (not to be confused with Oshun, the Orisha of rivers and sensuality). "You are reaching the age of responsibility, my son,"

Ogun as a young man

Obatala told Ogun one day. "Choose from one of the many available princesses, it is time you started a family!" Unfortunately, Ogun had fallen in love with his own mother, and of lately had convinced her to allow the unthinkable to happen. Each time Obatala was away, Ogun would overfeed Osun, giving him Eleggua's portion, which made the rooster fall asleep in a gluttonous stupor. Ogun would then lock Eleggua out of the house so he could have his way with Yemmu.

It wasn't long before Obatala noticed that Osun was becoming obese while Eleggua was looking emaciated. "What is going on, Eleggua?"—Obatala's booming voice showed deep concern—"Why are you so thin while the rooster is as big as a house?" "Oh, Father," a very sad Eleggua responded—"I wish I could spare you this pain, but I know that I have to tell you what's going on. Each time you go away, Ogun gives Osun my food, he then waits for the rooster to fall asleep in order to throw me out of the house, locking the doors so that I don't see what he is doing with Mother."

His enormous eyes filled with tears, yet Obatala said nothing, instead, he pretended to go away only to return after a few minutes. As Eleggua had said, Osun slept in a gluttonous stupor, while little Eleggua waited outside. Coming inside the house, Obaigbo faced the indescribable pain of seeing his beloved wife in shameful embrace with their firstborn. Obatala lifted his hand to curse Ogun, but the young man fell on his face in abject desolation, crying "Do not curse me. Father, for I curse myself, from now on I'll never feel the comfort of rest, for I'll toil incessantly every minute of my existence. The secret of making iron weapons and tools I'll give to the humans, so that not even the god of the forge will I be, and I'll go far away, where your holy gaze may never be soiled by looking into this wretched man." "So be it!," Obatala said. Looking at Yemmu, Baba said: "You I cannot curse, for it would be like cursing myself, but the next man child you have, I'll kill!" Turning to Osun, Obatala said: "Because you were not vigilant as my guardian should be, I'll give you to Eleggua, to always be his slave." "And to you, my son, who has suffered because of my inability to see what was happening, I give you the right to eat

Obatala sentencing Ogun

before anyone else, and the right to be propitiated first, before any other Orisha. Blessed be my son Eleggua forever more!"

Commentary: Out of a painful mistake of the gods, came the secret of the forge to humanity. This shows that even in the most awful circumstances, some of God's blessings may still be felt somewhere. Here we also see one of many explanations of why Eshu-Eleggua is the first Orisha to be propitiated.

Becoming extremely morose and wanting to flee the company of men and gods after his expulsion from his father's sight, Ogun hurriedly taught some lessons to humans on how to make iron implements, and then he left. Unfortunately, humans are not as able to retain information as Orisha, so they quickly forgot what Ogun had taught them. The iron tools and weapons humans made were defective, either very brittle or so soft as to be useless. Ogun by this time had left the civilized world, swearing never to return. When Obaigbo saw what had happened, he ordered that Ogun be brought back as soon as possible so humans could properly learn the secret of the forge. When Ogun was finally found, it seemed no one was able to convince him to return. Finally, Oshun, the young and beautiful Orisha of the rivers and goddess of sensuality asked Father Obaigbo for permission to try to bring Ogun back. "Ogun will not be able to resist my honey, Father," the salacious nymphet told Obatala. Although protective of his incredibly beautiful daughter, Obaigbo knew that if there was someone who could convince anybody to do anything, it was Oshun. Going to the river, Oshun took off her robes and rubbed honey all over her body. She had just discovered the secret of harvesting honey (oñi in Lukumi, oyin in Yoruba). By adding her own special ingredients to the viscous fluid, she made honey that was irresistibly delicious. Naked but for her bracelets and anklets, and carrying a big pot of her honey, Oshun went in search of Ogun. Hiding behind the foliage, the master hunter observed the stunning beauty as she seemingly without a worry in the world danced and laughed in the forest. Coming nearer, Ogun heard what Oshun was singing about:

Ogun of the Forge,

Ogun of the Hunt,

Ogun the Warrior without fear,

Are you scared of a little girl

With nothing on but a few bracelets?

Becoming enraged, Ogun jumped on Oshun, but she was ready for him. In one quick movement, Oshun passed her right hand full of honey over Ogun's lips. He had never tasted anything so sweet or delicious, so he sought to get more by attempting to grab Oshun. Oshun, however, slipped away from his hold and ran towards the city. Every few paces, Oshun would allow Ogun to grab her, but because she was slippery from all the honey she had rubbed on herself, she easily escaped. So intent was Ogun in grabbing Oshun, that he did not realize how close to the city he had been led. Finally, Ogun grabbed Oshun one more time, when he suddenly realized that he was surrounded by people. Embarrassed, he taught them properly, and promised to be available to workers of the forge as their protector whenever they needed him.

Commentary: Here we see an example, very common in Yoruba tradition, of a physically weaker being getting the best of a brawny one. Oshun's skill—her use of "feminine wile"—served to conquer one of the strongest of gods. The obvious allusion to female sexuality is also unmistakable, for even the most concrete thinker must be tempted to see in Oshun's honey an euphemism for her feminine allure. One of the proverbs that accompanies this pataki says, "you can catch more ants with a plate of honey than with a slingshot."

Ogun striking

Many years had passed by the time Shango was born to Yemmu and Baba. So beautiful was this child that Obatala didn't have the heart to kill him. Instead, he gave the bouncing baby boy to his daughter Dada, a warrior Orisha who lives on top of the Palm Tree. There, Dada raised Shango as her own, bringing him to spend time with the Old Man each day. Since Ogun's fall, Baba had not been the same. It seemed as if the only time a smile would light up Baba's noble face was when he was playing with Shango. Sadly, Yemmu could only see her son from a respectable distance, Baba not allowing her even to shake his hand. One day, when Shango was already a young adult, Baba told him about Ogun and Yemmu. A tear trickled down the cheek of the Greatest of all Orisha. Shango's pain was great. Now he understood why Baba was so sad all the time. "Baba, I want to avenge you. Tell me two things. Who is Ogun's wife, and where do they live?" Realizing that not even he could stand in the way of destiny, Baba told Shango where to find Ogun. "He lives with Oya at the far end of the forest," Obatala said. Shango vaguely remembered his fiery sister Oya, a tomboy who used to play warrior with the boys rather than house with the girls. "I have to leave, Father," Shango said. Without lifting his eyes, Obatala placed his hand on Shango's shoulder as he blessed him.

Mounting his beautiful white stallion, Eshinla, wearing his most gaudy royal robes, Shango presented an irresistible image. It wasn't long before Shango convinced Oya to leave Ogun and be with him. When Ogun came back from work—he worked all the time, stopping only to eat—he found his wife gone. People told him what had happened. This is where Ogun's enmity with Shango began.

Commentary: Although Shango was at first inspired by a desire to avenge his father's honor, he later grew to love Oya with all his heart, she becoming his perfect compliment, his favorite wife. This pataki shows that one's happiness may be found in most unexpected places.

A distraught Obatala tells his son Shango about Ogun's incest with his own mother.

After Oya left Ogun, he decided to go deep into the jungle where he could live by himself. Osanyin, who ruled over vegetation, welcomed Ogun to his domain. Observing how Ogun was a great pathfinder, but not a very accurate archer, Osanyin suggested that Ogun meet with Oshosi, god of the hunt, who also lived in the jungle. Oshosi was a great hunter, but he had trouble getting to his prey because he had difficulty finding his way among all of the thick vegetation. Ogun and Oshosi made a pact to hunt together, Oshosi never missing his mark, and Ogun easily finding it, making paths all over the forest. This was how Ogun and Oshosi became inseparable partners.

Commentary: This beautiful story shows how cooperation can result in better productivity. Both Ogun and Oshosi had special talents, but it was not until they combined their talents that maximum benefits were able to be reaped.

OGUNDA MEJI

African babalawo, such as the head babalawo, Wande Abimbola (, say that Ogun lives through the Odu Ifa called Ogunda Meji, which in the fixed order of the corpus occupied the ninth position. The material depiction of Ogunda Meji is the sabre or long machete which is a symbol of male strength and creativity, the power to forge metal into useful tools and weapons. Ogunda Meji is the tongue of Ogun, here he is said to be the clearer of paths, he is also depicted as Proud and enormous. This Odu also relates that Ogun led the second mission from heaven to earth as God's eyes and protection. That protection relates to the need to survive the physical body element created through Ogunda Meji.

- Ogunda Meji= Male Reproductive Organs.
- Children born under this Odu tend to be soldiers, butchers, iron workers, and burglars.

- This Odu denotes War
- This Odu denotes total victory (Ire)
- This Odu denotes total devastation (Osorbo)
- All of this person's good fortune is with his Ori.
- Keeps the law away (Ko Si Achelu), prevents surgery.
- Watch out not to be dominated by events and consequences.
- Children born under this Odu must become priests of Ogun or face death by violent accident.
- Without Ogun, no four-footed animal can be sacrificed, no infant's cord cut (separating him into individual life), nor the act of circumcision accomplished.
- In dilogun, the divination system employed by santeros, Ogunda is indicated by three cowries with open mouths.

Commentary: That is why, to this day, in traditional courts, one swears to Ogun like one swears to the Bible.

2

ATTRIBUTES

Necklace: Ogun's necklace alternates green and black beads. Sometimes they are grouped in groups of seven—seven green, seven black, until desired length is reached. An iron chain with miniature tools hanging from it is also used as a necklace by Ogun devotees sometimes.

Shrine (igbodu)—How initiates honor Ogun: Ogun's mysteries are usually kept inside a three-legged iron pot. Ogun's tools include a miniature anvil and six other miniature iron implements, a small iron bow-and-arrow, representing Ogun's inseparable friend and hunting partner Oshosi, two stones, one representing Ogun, the other Oshosi, plus three or six railroad spikes, three or six horseshoes, a pair of handcuffs, and any other iron miniature, such as representations of trains, of guns. A chain is sometimes tied around the pot in order to contain its energy, and a large machete or cutlass is always added to the mix as one of the most recognizable symbols of the Orisha.

Guerreros with offerings

The Warriors: The very serious initiation known as "The Warriors" is fundamental to anyone considering Santeria as his or her spiritual path. While having Warriors does not make anyone a priest or priestess, a person with Warriors can no longer consider himself or herself a client of a Santero or Santera, but a member of his or her community of believers. In fact, in Cuba, people who had Warriors and Initiatory Necklaces were considered "half seated" priests-to-be, the preliminary requirements of Guerreros and Collares having been met. Besides Ogun, who is represented by the iron pot with tools, and Oshosi, represented by the bow and arrow, the other two Orisha that make up The Warriors are Osun (not to be confused with Oshun, or with Osanyin), represented by a silver-colored chalice surmounted by a small metal rooster, and Eshu-Eleggua (Elegbara), which can have many different shapes, depending on the path that is needed. The most common is a cement cone about six inches high having eyes, nose, and mouth fashioned out of cowry shells, the whole "little head" resting on a terra-cotta dish, which brings to mind the Hindu god Shiva's representation as a phallic cement structure called lingham which rests on a receptacle called Yoni. It has been traditional in Cuban Santeria to have babalawo (priests of Ifa) make The Warriors or, at minimum, prepare the Osun. In this manner, most Santeria houses are linked to Ifa houses.

According to practitioners of Cuban Santeria, the priesthood of the babalawo is superior to that of the Santeros. In Brazil, however, babalawo are of little importance, the most powerful terreiros (congregations) in Bahia being actually led by women (Cuban babalawo have a taboo about ordaining women or gay men to their priesthood).

The Warriors—Eshu-Eleggua, Ogun, Oshosi, and Osun—are kept close to the main entrance of the home. Believers honor them with prayers and offerings every Monday, for this reason, anyone who has Warriors is by definition an active participant in Santeria. Neglecting to propitiate The Warriors on a weekly basis may cause a person to be held back from succeeding at a number of things, while keeping them happy facilitates a person's success.

"The Warriors"
Eleggua, Ogun, Oshosi, and (flying) Osun

Making Ogun: Initiation Shrine: When a son or daughter of Orisha Ogun becomes consecrated to his priesthood in a ceremony called kariocha (to seat on the head), two very specific shrines, called thrones, must be constructed; one outdoors, the other indoors. The outdoor shrine is rather rustic and unadorned, consisting of a tree stump big enough to allow the neophyte priest to sit on it. Almond trees are thought to be perfect, but a number of tree stumps are equally useful as thrones. A large stone that had been found in a wooded area is consecrated by washing it in omiero, a mixture of herbs that belong to Ogun with water and sacrificial blood, the sacrifice in question being that of a red rooster offered to the stone. The stone must be placed by the outdoor throne.

The throne indoors is much more sumptuous, recalling that Ogun is a king. Here, one can use one's imagination in using sequined black and green fabrics, combining them in an artistic fashion. The following artifacts must be present in the indoor throne, usually hanging from up high. A grass skirt such as those worn by "hula girls" (mariwo), hung opened behind the throne as a curtain, symbol of magic and the woods. A piece of white fabric about six feet square hung from the ceiling to look like the roof of a tent, this represents Obatala. A smoked jutia, which is a Cuban rodent about as big as a small cat, which looks like a possum. A smoked fish, seven gourds about the size of coconut (four painted green and black, three white and black), each containing the following: cocoa butter, powdered smoked fish, toasted corn, three foreign coins, and seven grains of black pepper. The throne room should be decorated with little bottles of liquor, like the ones they use in airlines, toy cars, toy guns, toy sabers etc.

Shrine (olujo alejo)—How non-initiates may begin to honor Ogun: The most often-used implement used by non-priests in Nigeria to represent Ogun is a machete, saber, cutlass, sword or large knife. In Cuba many people honor Ogun's Catholic disguises, variously thought of as John the Baptist or St.. Peter.

WARNING: DO NOT JUST BUY AN OGUN POT WITH IMPLEMENTS AT A BOTANICA AND PLACE IT BEHIND DOOR WITHOUT THEM BEING PROPERLY PREPARED BY BONA FIDE PRIESTHOOD HOLDERS.

As this is very dangerous, unwanted spirits often hiding in the unconsecrated pot. A small incense burner in the shape of a three-legged pot, however, is acceptable as a focus of veneration, as are toy cars made of metal, or choo-choo trains.

Offerings (adimu): He loves hot spices, such as chili peppers, and roasted African yams. He favors hard liquor, including rum and gin. His tools are rubbed with palm oil. Honey may be occasionally offered him to sweeten his disposition. (It reminds him of his tenderness with Oshun).

Blood Offerings (ebó): Traditionally, the Warriors are offered a goat for Eleggua, Ogun, and Oshosi, a pigeon for Ogun (any color), the same for Oshosi, and a totally white dove or pigeon for Osun. Ogun also likes guinea fowl and roosters.

Herbs and plants: Black Poppy, Hyssop, Oak Tree, Birch, Groundsil, Snakeweed, Teasel, Navew, Mariwo, Alligator Pepper, Eucalyptis.

Characteristics of Ogun (and of his devotees): Ogun's Catholic disguise is usually as St. Peter and, sometimes, as John the Baptist. His feast day in Cuba is celebrated on June 29th. Ogun's colors are green and black (in Africa, very dark blue—the color of work clothes in Nigeria). His numbers are three and seven. When three shells fall face up in the Dilogun oracle, it is called "Ogunda," where Ogun speaks, and the accompanying refrain is " where tragedy began," alluding to the tragedy of Ogun's incest with his mother. Ogun is the patron Orisha of anyone who works with iron or steel, as Ogun Ode Mata, he is Oshosi's inseparable companion and protects hunters. Ogun also protects gunslingers, guerrillas, and all soldiers. He is a god of war and of fighting, yet he is also the god of surgeons and medicine men and women. Ogun's most striking characteristic is his indefatigable stamina. His children, as those born with Ogun in their heads are called, tend to be hard workers, non-quitters, very serious about their careers. Ogun's children tend to be physically strong, but prone to alcoholism. They can be tactless in their desire to be frank and totally honest.

ROADS OF OGUN:

Ogun Alake: Ogun of the hunters, eats dogs.

Ogun Ajero: Eats ram.

Ogun Seriki: Eats dogs.

Ogun Melemele: Eats roasted yam.

Ogun Isono: Eats snails.

Ogun Irano: The bloodthirsty path.

Ogun Oloola: The Lord of the body artists.

Ogun Ikola: The protector of surgeons.

Ogun Onigbajamo: The protector of barbers.

Ogun Alapata: Eats raw meat.

Ogun Gbenagbena: Accepts tree sap as offering.

Ogun Niwe, Nile: Syncretized with St. John the Baptist.

Ogundeka.

Ogun Ode Mata: The One who walks with Oshosi.

Laibé.

Obaniyi.

Weriweri.

Arere: St. Peter or St. Paul.

Chibirikí: St. Michael the archangel.

Alailuó: Gabriel the archangel.

Ara.

Atamatesí.

Alawedé.

Dade.

Sarabanda, Zarabanda: Ogun's name in Palo, where he is one of the top three deities worshipped.

Lamá.

Roads in Africa: According to E. Bolaji Idowu, writing in his classic book Olódùmarè, God in Yoruba Belief (Plainview, N.Y.: Original Publications, 1994) page 86, Ogun has seven "designations" in Yorubaland, these are:

Ogun Onire: Lord of Iré.

Ogun Alara: Lord of dogs.

Ogun Ikola: Lord of medicine and circumsicion.

Ogun Elemona: Lord of Yams.

Ogun Akirin: Lord of Rams.

Ogun gbena-gbena: Lord of Artisans.

Ogun makinde: Lord of the outdoors.

Ogun in Haiti: In Haiti Ogun (Papa Ogou) is extremely important. Interestingly, there they consider Shango to be a path of Ogun!

Ogun in Brazil: Also syncretized with St. Peter and St. Paul, as well as with St. Anthony, Orixa Ogum holds a position in Afro-Brazilian religions as important as he does in Cuba. The story of Oya leaving him for Shango (Xango) is also known in Brazil. He is thought to have seven "roads" in Brazil: Onire, Alagbede, Ja, Omini, Wari, Erotondo, and Akoro Onigbe. In Brazil, his color is red and, also, dark blue and green. His day is Tuesday. He is offered oxen and goats. He is described as aggressive and brutal, but also as the orixa of technology. He is identified with brutal honesty and hard work. In Brazil, Ogun's children are not permitted to drink hard liquors or carry knives.

Initiation names: I recently wrote about the predicament I saw an oriaté endure: when it came time to give a neophyte priest he was initiating a sacred name, each name the oriate proposed, the Orisha being seated refused to accept, then the oriate ran out of names! Luckily, a couple of us old dinosaurs remembered enough appropriate names to come up with one the Orisha liked. The following traditional Lukumi names given to those who become priests and priestesses of Ogun were published by the learned elder Andres Hing in 1971, unfortunately, his self-published book has been out of print for many years.

Ogun bi; Ogun ronke; Ogun wande; Ogun tolu; Ogun fonsho; Ogun baloguyeye; Ogundei; Ogun lawo; Ogun toye; Ogun lana; Ogun fumito; Ogun leti; Ogun nike; Ogun niwe; Ogun Laibe; Ogun Oka; Ogun Meji; Ogun ibite;Ogun lode; Ogunde; Ogun levi; Ogun onile; Ogun olue; Ogun ora; Ogun wama; Ogun talue.

3

OGUN AND SANTERIA'S "CELESTIAL COURT"

As one of The Warriors, one of Santeria's defining initiations, Ogun is of enormous importance, for the Warriors are thought to be the Orisha that protect and guard the home against physical as well as spiritual dangers. As one of the four Warrior Orisha, Ogun is worshipped by ALL who practice Santeria. Along with Eleggua, Oshosi, and Osun, Ogun receives almost constant attention, as all Practitioners are supposed to worship the Warriors on Mondays or Tuesdays (Monday is Eleggua's day, Tuesday is Ogun's).

Although in Santeria hagiography Ogun is depicted as having the sad distinction of bringing imbalance to the world by falling in love with his own mother, his dogged adherence to the truth, his noble character, and his unswerving devotion to hard work make Ogun an extremely accessible Orisha.

Ogun lives apart from the other Orisha, except Oshosi, Eleggua, and Osun, his partners. In the Celestial court he is thought of as both pariah and indispensable king. His ambiguous role as both sinner and saint mirrors the constant struggle human beings face to do what's right while being bombarded with temptations. Usually pictured as a strong, hard man, our hearts go out to Ogun when pretty boy Shango sweeps his wife off her feet. There must be many who have suffered as Ogun did.

Not that Ogun is described as ugly; just average, like most people are. Shango used his above-average looks to tempt Oya. Ogun, a god, had to face what millions of men and women face, losing a loved one to another person. In this, the god of iron showed his deepest humanity.

Ogun's place in Santeria's Celestial Court is unique. As a member of the Orisha quartet know as The Warriors, the amount of worship Ogun receives is unparalleled, except by Eleggua, his fellow warrior.

4

ORIKI OGUN: ORIN OGUN
PRAYERS AND SONGS TO OGUN

In Cuba, it is said that when we talk to the Orisha in their own language, it makes them better disposed to grant our petition. Priesthood holders are expected to learn the songs and praises to the Orisha in Lukumi, an archaic form of Yoruba that developed in Cuba. Because Yoruba is a tonal language, and in Cuba the Lukumi did not develop a system of writing down the different tonalities, Lukumi songs and prayers are often hard to render into standard Yoruba. John Mason, a priest of Obatala operating out of Brooklyn, New York, has dedicated a great deal of time and effort to render Lukumi songs into standard Yoruba, a laudable effort. The word "Ogun," for example, with its appropriate accents, can mean anything from war to medicine! Add to that the fact that the Yoruba love to pun, and you find yourself with a very hard task when trying to decipher these songs. The effort we make in trying to sing these praises to our beloved Orisha, however, does not go unnoticed by them. I think the Orisha must be pleased that we are at least trying!

Oriki Ogun

Ògún Aládàá méji: óñ fi 'kan sán ko,
ó ñ fi'kan yè nà
Ògún Onílé owó, olónà olà, onílé kángun-
kàngun ònà òrun.
Awón l' éyin'jú ègbè léyin omo òrukàn,
onílé Kángun-Kàngun ònà òrun.
Òrisà tí ó wípé ti Ògún kò tó nnkan, ááf owó
je' su nígbà àimoye.

Ogun the possessor of two machetes;
With one he prepares the farm,
And with the other he clears the road
Ogun, the owner of the house of money,
The owner of the house of riches,
The owner of the innumerable houses of heaven.
One whose eyeballs are rare to behold,
Support behind the orphan,
The owner of the innumerable houses of heaven.
Whichever Orisha regards Ogun as of no consequence,
Let him eat his yams with his hands,
Without a knife, each time, forevermore.[4]

5

Despojos: Cleansings with Ogun

A very popular, simple, yet effective cleansing with Ogun involves buying a cheap cut of meat, rubbing palm oil on it, then ritualistically passing it around your body—you don't need to actually touch your body with the meat, just pass it about an inch away, it will pick up all the negative energy you have. After doing this, go to a railroad track or subway station, and leave meat by tracks with seven pennies. Some people say that if you do this operation on an automobile you wish to sell, Ogun will help you sell it quickly.

A large white African yam, baked for an hour, is a favorite food of Ogun. Because Ogun is a hunter who lives in the forest, he doesn't usually eat fancy foods, he likes his food simple and unadorned. All game animals are enjoyed by Ogun, as are rabbits.

Anyone who has The Warriors should know that writing the names of your enemies on parchment or brown paper bag and putting the paper either inside or under Ogun's pot is enough to keep them at bay.

An antidote to prevent black magic or psychic attacks is made by invoking Ogun's help, grinding some yucca (potato-like tuber sold wherever Cubans or Puerto Ricans live), okra, ashes, water, and menstrual blood, mixing all of these ingredients, and throwing it where you suspect the attack has occurred, i.e., your front door. Lydia Cabrera in El Monte, page 563, calls this remedy "the most efficacious protection against witchcraft."

The following cleansing is said to prevent tragedies. Take three yards of red material, three buckets filled with fresh water, thirteen slugs (slimy creatures that look like leeches), three caterpillars taken from a palm tree. Cleanse yourself in front of Ogun's pot with all ingredients. Leave bundle, along with three pennies, by a railroad track.

Cooking for Ogun is simple. He enjoys meat fried in palm oil, all kinds of beans, just boiled or raw. And African white yams (called ñames in Spanish-speaking areas), especially if roasted.

END NOTES

1. Ulli Beier, *Yoruba Poetry* (Cambridge: Cambridge University Press, 1970) p.34.

2. Sandra T. Barnes, *Africa's Ogun* (Bloomington, Indiana: Indiana University Press, 1997) p. xiv.

3. Wande Abimbola, *Ifa Will Mend Our Broken World* (Roxbury, Mass: Aim Books, 1997) p.70. Note that in Cuban Santeria there is no mention of Ajala, Obatala being the creator of the Ori.

4. E. Bolaji Idowu, *Olodumare, God in Yoruba Belief* (Plainview N.Y.: Original Publications, 1995) p. 85.

ITEM #001
$14.95

SANTERIA

AFRICAN MAGIC IN LATIN AMERICA

BY MIGENE GONZALEZ WIPPLER

In 1973, the first hardcover edition of *Santeria: African Magic in Latin America* by cultural anthropologist Migene Gonzalez-Wippler was first published by Julian Press. It became an immediate best-seller and is still considered by many experts one of the most popular books on Santeria, having gone through 4 editions and several translations. Now this beloved classic, written by one the foremost scholars on the Afro-Cuban religion, has returned in a 5th edition. This time the text has been carefully edited and corrected to incorporate vital new material. The beliefs, practices, legends of Santeria are brilliantly brought to life in this exciting and critically acclaimed best-seller. If you ever wondered what Santeria is, if you are curious about the rituals and practices of this mysterious religion, and want to delve in its deepest secrets, this book will answer all your questions and much more.

ISBN 0-942272-04-8 5½"x 8½" $14.95

Item #002
$14.95

THE SANTERIA EXPERIENCE

Migene Gonzalez Wippler

"The Santeria Experience is an autobiographical account of initiation into a clandestinely-practiced religion. Ms. Gonzalez Wippler rewards her readers with the raw emotional impact of her personal encounters with the religion as both a researcher and an initiate. She is the first writer to present to an English-speaking audience the full emotional impact and ritual complexities of Santeria."

- From Foreword by Andres Perez y Mena

"The Santeria Experience fills an important need for a definitive treatise about a religio-magical cult that reputedly has millions of indoctrinated followers in the Caribbean Islands, South America, and Latin American sectors of the United States. Migene Gonzalez Wippler is a brilliant narrator whose vivid firsthand descriptions of exotic rituals will be instructive and fascinating to professional and lay persons alike. Replete with a comprehensive glossary and bibliography, this book should provide a rewarding experience for all who are intrigued by the advantages and pitfalls of this widespread, mind expanding phenomenon."

- Stanley R. Dean, M.D. Psychiatry and Mysticism

ISBN 0-942272-15-3 5½"x 8½" 228 pages $14.95

Item #003
$9.95

RITUALS AND SPELLS OF SANTERIA

Migene Gonzalez Wippler

Santeria is an earth religion. That is, it is a magico-religious system that has its roots in nature and natural forces. Each orisha or saint is identified with a force of nature and with a human interest or endeavor. Chango, for instance, is the god of fire, thunder and lightning, but he is also the symbol of justice and protects his followers against enemies. He also symbolizes passion and virility and is often invoked in works of seduction. Oshun, on the other hand, symbolizes river waters, love and marriage. She is essentially the archetype of joy and pleasure. Yemaya is identified with the seven seas, but is also the symbol of Motherhood and protects women in their endeavors. Eleggua symbolizes the crossroads, and is the orisha of change and destiny, the one who makes things possible or impossible. He symbolizes the balance of things. Obatala is the father, the symbol of peace and purity. Oya symbolizes the winds and is the owner of the cemetery, the watcher of the doorway between life and death. She is not death, but the awareness of its existence. Oggun is the patron of all metals, and protects farmers, carpenters, butchers, surgeons, mechanics, and all who work with or near metals. He also rules over accidents, which he often causes.

ISBN 0-942272-07-2 5½"x 8½" 134 pages $9.95